THE
LILIAN S. BESORE
MEMORIAL LIBRARY
GREENCASTLE, PENNSYLVANIA
FOUNDED MARCH 20, 1963

CONOCOCHEAGUE DISTRICT LIBRARY
102 NORTH MAIN STREET
CHAMBERSBURG, PENNSYLVANIA 17201

LILIAN S. BESORE MEMORIAL LIBRARY
305 E. BALTIMORE ST.
GREENCASTLE, PA. 17225